SHADOW WARRIORS
The Wagner Group

Written by:
Sahil A Gosalia

SHADOW WARRIORS

The Wagner Group

Sahil A Gosalia

Copyright © 2023 by Sahil A Gosalia

All rights reserved. No part of this book may be reproduced or transmitted in any form or by any means, electronic or mechanical, including photocopying, recording, or by any information storage and retrieval system, without written permission from the author, except for the inclusion of brief quotations in a review.

The characters and events portrayed in this book are fictitious. Any similarity to real persons, living or dead, is coincidental and not intended by the author.

Cover design by Sahil A Gosalia

Published by: Independently Published

Foreword

The Wagner Group has become a prominent name in the world of private military contractors, known for their secretive operations and close association with the Russian government. As the world becomes increasingly aware of their activities, it is important to understand the history and motivations behind this controversial organization.

In this book, author Sahil A Gosalia provides a comprehensive analysis of the Wagner Group, from its origins to its current global reach. Gosalia delves into their military operations in Ukraine and Syria, as well as their resource extraction in Africa and political interference in Sudan. He also explores their relationship with the Russian government, controversies and criticisms, and the group's future ambitions.

This book is not only informative but also eye-opening, revealing the often-hidden world of private military contractors and their impact on regional and international security. I highly recommend this book to anyone interested in understanding the complex web of global politics and the role of private military contractors in shaping it.

S. Gosalia

Sahil A Gosalia

(Author)

This book is dedicated to *all readers who share a fascination for the world of espionage, covert operations, and the intricate workings of global politics. To those who seek to understand the complexities of international relations, and the hidden machinations that shape our world, this book is for you.*

I hope that the insights and revelations provided within these pages will serve to enlighten and educate, entertain and enthrall, and to spark a greater understanding and appreciation for the forces that shape our world.

May this book inspire you to delve deeper into the mysteries of the world around us, and to uncover the secrets that lie just beyond our grasp. For those who share my fascination for writing suspenseful and futuristic stories, I dedicate this book to you, with the hope that it will spark your imagination and inspire you to continue exploring the limitless possibilities of the human mind.

"**Shadow Warfare: Wagner Group**" is a book that sheds light on one of the world's most controversial and secretive private military and security companies. This book delves into the origins and expansion of the Wagner Group, its involvement in conflicts and operations worldwide, and the controversies and criticism surrounding the group.

This book offers a comprehensive and in-depth look at the Wagner Group's activities and is a valuable resource for anyone seeking to understand the complex and shadowy world of private military and security companies. It offers insights into the group's motivations, tactics, and strategies, as well as its relationship with the Russian government and its impact on global security.

Additionally, this book highlights the challenges and criticisms facing private military and security companies and raises important questions about their role in global conflicts and operations. It offers a nuanced and balanced perspective on the Wagner Group and provides readers with a better understanding of the risks and implications of such groups for international security and stability.

Overall, "Shadow Warfare: Wagner Group" is a must-read for anyone interested in the world of private military and security companies and those seeking to understand the complex and evolving nature of global security in the 21st century.

Table of Contents

Chapter 1: The Founding of the Wagner Group

The Wagner Group is a private military company (PMC) that was founded in 2014 by Yevgeny Prigozhin, a Russian businessman with close ties to President Vladimir Putin. The company's original purpose was to provide security and training services for Russian businesses operating in conflict zones, such as Syria and Ukraine.

Chapter 2: The Wagner Group's Activities in Ukraine

The Wagner Group gained international attention in 2014 when it became involved in the conflict in Ukraine. The company sent mercenaries to fight alongside Russian-backed separatists in the Donbas region of eastern Ukraine. The group's involvement in Ukraine was initially denied by the Russian government, but evidence later emerged that proved its presence.

Chapter 3: The Wagner Group's Activities in Syria

In 2015, the Wagner Group began providing military support to the regime of Syrian President Bashar al-Assad. The group's fighters were involved in some of the most intense battles of the Syrian conflict, including the siege of Aleppo. Wagner Group fighters have also been accused of committing war crimes, including the execution of prisoners of war.

Chapter 4: The Group's Activities in Africa

This chapter explores the Wagner Group's activities in Africa, including its military operations in Libya, resource extraction in the Central African Republic, and political interference in Sudan. The chapter also examines the implications of the group's activities for regional security and international relations.

Chapter 5: The Wagner Groups' Role in Russian Policy

The chapter focuses on the Wagner Group's relationship with the Russian government and its role in Russian foreign policy. It explores the extent to which the Russian state controls or supports the group, and how its activities align with Russian interests. The chapter also examines the implications of the group's relationship with the state, including its potential impact on Russia's international reputation and relations with other countries.

Chapter 6: The Wagner Group's Expansion and Global Reach

This chapter delves into the Wagner Group's expansion and global reach beyond its origins in Russia and Ukraine. It explores the group's activities in various regions, including the Middle East, Africa, and South America, and examines its motivations for expanding its operations. The chapter also explores the potential risks and challenges of the group's global reach, including the impact on regional stability and its potential to provoke conflict with other countries.

Chapter 7: The Wagner Group's Relationship with the Russian Government

The chapter analyzes the Wagner Group's relationship with the Russian government, including the extent to which the group operates with the government's knowledge and support. The chapter explores the potential implications of the group's relationship with the government for Russia's foreign policy objectives and its relations with other countries. It also examines the role that the Wagner Group plays in the context of Russia's broader geopolitical strategies and ambitions.

Chapter 8: Controversies and Criticisms

Chapter 8 scrutinizes the controversies and criticisms

surrounding the Wagner Group. It explores the allegations of human rights violations, war crimes, and illegal activities that have been levelled against the group. The chapter also examines the group's potential impact on regional and international stability, as well as the political and diplomatic consequences of its actions. Finally, it discusses the ethical and moral implications of private military companies like the Wagner Group operating outside of state control.

Chapter 9: Current Status and Future Prospects

The chapter evaluates the current status and future prospects of the Wagner Group. It assesses the group's current activities and potential future operations, as well as the challenges and opportunities it faces. The chapter also discusses the group's potential impact on global security and the geopolitical implications of its activities. Finally, it explores possible scenarios for the group's future development, including potential regulatory frameworks and geopolitical constraints.

Trajectory

The trajectory and timeline of the Wagner Group is a complex and evolving story. It began as a small security company in Russia and quickly grew into a major player in conflicts around the world, with involvement in Ukraine, Syria, Libya, and Africa. The group's close relationship with the Russian government has also been a key factor in its rise to prominence.

However, controversies and criticisms have also surrounded the group's activities, raising questions about its prospects and impact on global security.

Chapter 1: The Founding of the Wagner Group

The Wagner Group is a private military company (PMC) that was founded in 2014 by Yevgeny Prigozhin, a Russian businessman with close ties to President Vladimir Putin. The company's original purpose was to provide security and training services for Russian businesses operating in conflict zones, such as Syria and Ukraine.

The origins of the Wagner Group can be traced back to the early 2010s when Prigozhin began to establish himself as a major player in the Russian defense industry. Prigozhin had made his fortune through a series of successful ventures, including a chain of restaurants and catering services that became popular with the Russian elite.

In 2012, Prigozhin established a new company called Concord Management and Consulting. The company was initially involved in providing catering services to the Russian military, but it soon expanded into other areas, including security and logistics. Prigozhin also began to develop close ties with the Russian government, particularly with officials in the Ministry of Defense and the Kremlin.

By 2014, Prigozhin had established a network of companies and personnel that were ready to take on new challenges. It was at this point that he decided to establish the Wagner Group.

The name "Wagner" was reportedly inspired by the German composer Richard Wagner, who was admired by both Prigozhin and Putin. The group's logo, a black sun, was also reportedly inspired by a Nazi symbol.

The Wagner Group's initial mission was to provide security services for Russian businesses operating in conflict zones, particularly in Ukraine and Syria. The company recruited former Russian soldiers and other personnel with experience in combat and security operations.

The Wagner Group's early operations were shrouded in secrecy. The company operated under several different names and was not officially registered with the Russian government. The group's fighters wore unmarked uniforms and did not carry identification.

The Wagner Group's first major deployment was in eastern Ukraine, where Russian-backed separatists had seized control of the Donbas region. The group's fighters, who were reportedly paid up to $1,500 per month, were tasked with providing security for separatist leaders and helping to train local militias.

The Wagner Group's involvement in Ukraine was initially denied by the Russian government, but evidence later emerged that proved its presence. In 2015, several Wagner Group fighters were captured by Ukrainian forces and subsequently tried and convicted for their role in the conflict.

Despite the setbacks in Ukraine, the Wagner Group continued to expand its operations. In 2015, the group began providing military support to the regime of Syrian President Bashar al-Assad. The group's fighters were involved in some of the most intense battles of the Syrian conflict, including the siege of Aleppo.

The Wagner Group's involvement in Syria was more overt than its activities in Ukraine. The group's fighters wore uniforms with the Wagner Group logo and were sometimes seen driving vehicles with the same logo. The group also established a training camp in the Syrian desert, where it trained Syrian soldiers and other pro-government forces.

The Wagner Group's involvement in Syria has been controversial. The group has been accused of committing war crimes, including the execution of prisoners of war. The group has also been linked to several incidents where civilians were killed or injured.

Despite the controversy, the Wagner Group continued to expand its operations. In 2018, the group was linked to mercenary activity in several African countries, including Sudan, Libya, and the Central African Republic. The group was also reportedly involved in Venezuela, where it provided security for President Nicolas Maduro.

The Wagner Group's ties to the Russian government have been the subject of much speculation. While the group operates as a private company, several of its leaders, including founder Yevgeny Prigozhin.

In 2018, the group was linked to mercenary activity in several African countries, including Sudan, Libya, and the Central African Republic. The group was also reportedly involved in Venezuela, where it provided security for President Nicolas Maduro.

The Wagner Group's ties to the Russian government have been the subject of much speculation. While the group operates as a private company, several of its leaders, including founder Yevgeny Prigozhin, have close ties to the Kremlin. Prigozhin, who is often referred to as "Putin's chef" due to his catering businesses, has been sanctioned by the US government for his alleged involvement in Russian interference in the 2016 US election.

The Russian government has denied any direct involvement with the Wagner Group, but many experts believe that the group is closely tied to Russian military intelligence, known as the GRU. The group's fighters are often equipped with Russian-made weapons and equipment, and some have been identified as active-duty soldiers in the Russian military.

The Wagner Group's operations have had a significant impact on conflicts around the world. In Ukraine, the group's involvement has prolonged the conflict and contributed to the deaths of thousands of people. In Syria, the group has helped the Assad regime regain control of large areas of the country but has also been accused of committing war crimes.

Despite the controversy surrounding the group, the Wagner Group continues to operate and expand its operations. In 2019, the group was linked to the killing of three Russian journalists in the Central African Republic. The journalists were investigating the group's activities in the country when they were ambushed and killed by unknown assailants.

The Wagner Group's activities have also attracted the attention of other countries. In 2018, the US military reportedly killed several Wagner Group fighters in a battle in Syria. The US government has accused the group of being a destabilizing force in several countries and has sanctioned several individuals and entities associated with the group.

In conclusion, the Wagner Group is a private military company that was founded in 2014 by Yevgeny Prigozhin. The group's initial mission was to provide security services for Russian businesses operating in conflict zones, but it has since expanded its operations to include military support for

Russian-backed regimes in Syria and other countries. The group's ties to the Russian government have been the subject of much speculation, and the group has been linked to several incidents of violence and war crimes. Despite the controversy, the Wagner Group continues to operate and expand its operations, and its impact on conflicts around the world is likely to continue for years to come.

Chapter 2: The Wagner Group's Activities in Ukraine

The Wagner Group first gained prominence in Ukraine, where it played a significant role in the ongoing conflict in the eastern part of the country. The group's involvement in Ukraine has been the subject of much controversy and speculation, and many questions remain unanswered about its activities in the country.

Origins of the Conflict in Eastern Ukraine

The Wagner Group's involvement in the conflict in eastern Ukraine can be traced back to the events that led up to the conflict, as well as the involvement of the Russian government in the conflict.

The origins of the conflict in eastern Ukraine can be traced back to the ousting of Ukrainian President Viktor Yanukovych in February

2014. Yanukovych, who had close ties to Russia, was forced to flee the country following widespread protests against his government.

Following Yanukovych's ousting, pro-Russian separatists in the Donetsk and Luhansk regions of Ukraine declared independence and began fighting against Ukrainian government forces. The separatists were supported by Russia, which provided them with military, economic, and political support.

Russia's involvement in the conflict in eastern Ukraine has been a subject of much debate and controversy. While Russia has denied any direct involvement in the conflict, there is substantial evidence to suggest that the country has provided significant support to the separatists.

One of the most significant forms of support provided by Russia to the separatists has been military support. Russian troops have been spotted fighting alongside the separatists in eastern Ukraine, and Russia has been accused of providing weapons and other military equipment to the separatists.

In addition to military support, Russia has also been accused of providing political and economic support to the separatists. The country has recognized the independence of the Donetsk and Luhansk regions and has provided them with economic and humanitarian aid.

In this context, the Wagner Group became involved in the conflict in eastern Ukraine. The group's founder, Dmitry Utkin, traveled to the region as a volunteer fighter in 2014, quickly rising to prominence among the Russian volunteers in the area. He began organizing and training them into a more cohesive fighting force.

In the fall of 2014, Utkin founded a private military company called "Patriot" with the support of Yevgeny Prigozhin, a wealthy businessman with close ties to Russian President Vladimir Putin. Patriot initially provided security services to Russian businesses operating in eastern Ukraine, but it soon began providing military support to the separatists.

In early 2015, Patriot was renamed the Wagner Group, and it began operating as a private military company, providing military support to the separatists in eastern Ukraine. The group's fighters were often seen alongside separatist forces in the region, and they played a significant role in several major battles.

The Wagner Group's involvement in the conflict in eastern Ukraine was characterized by a high degree of secrecy and deniability. The group's fighters operated under false identities and were forbidden from discussing their activities with anyone outside the group. The group's leadership also remained largely unknown, with Utkin and Prigozhin denying any direct involvement with the group.

The Wagner Group's involvement in the conflict in eastern Ukraine was not without controversy. The group was accused of committing human rights abuses, including torture and extrajudicial killings. The group was also accused of involvement in the downing of Malaysian Airlines Flight 17 in July 2014, which was shot down over eastern Ukraine, killing all 298 people on board.

Russia's Involvement in the Conflict

Russia's involvement in the conflict in eastern Ukraine has been a subject of much debate and controversy. While Russia has denied any direct involvement in the conflict, there is substantial evidence to suggest that the country has provided significant support to the separatists.

One of the most significant forms of support provided by Russia to the separatists has been military support. Russian troops have been spotted fighting alongside the separatists in eastern Ukraine, and Russia has been accused of providing weapons and other military equipment to the separatists.

In addition to military support, Russia has also been accused of providing political and economic support to the separatists. The country has recognized the independence of the Donetsk and Luhansk regions and has provided them with economic and humanitarian aid.

Here are some specific details of the group's activities in eastern Ukraine:

- The Wagner Group first became involved in the conflict in eastern Ukraine in 2014. The group's fighters were primarily deployed to the Donetsk and Luhansk regions, where they fought alongside separatist rebels.

- The group's fighters were involved in numerous battles and skirmishes in eastern Ukraine, including the battle for Donetsk airport in 2014 and the battle for Debaltseve in 2015.
- The Wagner Group's fighters played a key role in supporting separatist rebels by providing infantry support, artillery fire, and intelligence gathering.

- The group's fighters were accused of committing numerous human rights cases of abuse in eastern Ukraine, including torture, extrajudicial killings, and looting. Human rights organizations and journalists have documented several instances of the group's fighters committing atrocities against Ukrainian civilians and prisoners of war.

- The Wagner Group was also involved in supplying weapons and military equipment to separatist rebels. The group reportedly supplied rebels with tanks, artillery, and other heavy weapons, which helped to tilt the balance of power in favour of the separatists.

- The group's involvement in the conflict in eastern Ukraine was controversial, with the Ukrainian government accusing the group of being a Russian military unit and violating Ukraine's territorial integrity. However, the Russian government denied any involvement in the conflict and maintained that the Wagner Group was a private military company.

- The Wagner Group's activities in eastern Ukraine had wider implications for Russia's foreign policy, with some analysts arguing that the group's involvement in the conflict was part of a broader strategy to undermine Ukraine's sovereignty and expand Russia's sphere of influence in the region.

Overall, the Wagner Group's activities in eastern Ukraine were primarily focused on providing military support to separatist rebels. The group's involvement in the conflict was controversial, with accusations of human rights abuses and wider implications for Russia's foreign policy in the region.

In conclusion, the Wagner Group's involvement in the conflict in eastern Ukraine can be seen as a part of Russia's wider involvement in the conflict. The group provided military support to the separatists, playing a significant role in the conflict in the region. However, the group's involvement in the conflict was characterized by a high degree of secrecy and deniability, and the full extent of its activities in the region remains unclear.

Chapter 3: The Wagner Group's Activities in Syria

The Wagner Group's involvement in the conflict in Syria began in 2015 when Russia began providing military support to the Syrian government in its fight against rebel forces. The group played a significant role in this support, providing military training, equipment, and personnel to the Syrian government.

The Wagner Group's involvement in Syria was largely driven by economic interests. The group saw an opportunity to profit from the conflict by providing military support to the Syrian government, which would allow it to secure lucrative contracts for the reconstruction of the country after the conflict was over.

The Wagner Group's activities in Syria were characterized by a high degree of secrecy and deniability. The group's fighters operated under false identities and were forbidden from discussing their activities with anyone outside the group. The group's leadership also remained largely unknown, with its founder, Dmitry Utkin, denying any direct involvement with the group.

The group's activities in Syria were also controversial. The group was accused of committing human rights abuses, including torture and extrajudicial killings. It was also accused of operating outside of the control of the Russian military, leading to concerns about the group's loyalty and its potential impact on Russia's wider foreign policy.

Despite these concerns, the Wagner Group continued to play a significant role in the conflict in

Syria. The group's fighters were involved in several major battles, including the battle for Palmyra in 2016 and the battle for Deir ez-Zor in 2017.

The group's involvement in the conflict in Syria was also marked by several high-profile incidents. In February 2018, a group of Wagner Group fighters were killed in a U.S. airstrike in Deir ez-Zor. The incident led to a public debate in Russia about the group's activities in Syria, with some criticizing the group for operating outside of the control of the Russian military.

In addition to its military activities, the Wagner Group was also involved in economic activities in Syria. The group secured several lucrative contracts for the reconstruction of the country after the conflict was over, including contracts for the reconstruction of Palmyra and Aleppo.

The group's involvement in the economic reconstruction of Syria was controversial, with some accusing the group of profiting from the conflict and exacerbating the humanitarian crisis in the country. However, the group defended its activities, arguing that it was providing much-needed support to the Syrian government and the people of Syria.

The Group's involvement in the conflict in Syria was characterized by a high degree of secrecy and deniability. The group played a significant role in providing military support to the Syrian government, and it also secured lucrative contracts for the reconstruction of the country after the conflict was over. However, the group's activities in Syria were controversial, with concerns about human rights abuses and the group's impact on Russia's wider foreign policy.

The Wagner Group's activities in Syria were diverse and included military, economic, and political activities. Here are some specific details of the group's activities in Syria:

Military Activities:

- The Wagner Group deployed several hundred fighters to Syria, who were involved in combat operations against rebel forces. The group's fighters operated under the cover of a private military company and were primarily involved in providing infantry support to the Syrian army.

- The Wagner Group played a key role in the retaking of Palmyra from ISIS in March 2016. According to reports, the group's fighters were involved in the offensive alongside Syrian government troops, and they played a significant role in the capture of the city.

- The group's fighters were also involved in the battle for Deir ez-Zor in September 2017. According to reports, the Wagner Group's fighters played a critical role in breaking the ISIS siege of the city and securing the airport.

- The group's fighters were also involved in other major battles in Syria, including the battle for Aleppo in 2016 and the battle for Raqqa in 2017.

Economic Activities:

- The Wagner Group secured several lucrative contracts for the reconstruction of Syria after the conflict was over. These contracts included the reconstruction of the Palmyra amphitheater, which was destroyed by ISIS, and the reconstruction of the Aleppo airport.

- The group's economic activities in Syria were controversial, with some accusing the group of profiting from the conflict and exacerbating the humanitarian crisis in the country. However, the group defended its activities, arguing that it was providing much-needed support to the Syrian government and the people of Syria.

Political Activities:

- The Wagner Group was involved in political activities in Syria, including negotiating with local tribes and opposition groups. The group reportedly played a key role in negotiating a ceasefire in southern Syria in 2017.

- The group was also involved in efforts to form a new Syrian government, with its fighters reportedly serving as advisors to the Syrian government on matters related to security and governance.

- The Wagner Group's political activities in Syria were controversial, with some accusing the group of undermining efforts to find a political solution to the conflict.

Overall, the group played a significant role in providing military support to the Syrian government, and it also secured lucrative contracts for the reconstruction of the country after the conflict was over. However, the group's activities in Syria were also controversial, with concerns about human rights abuses, its impact on Russia's wider foreign policy, and its involvement in political activities.

Chapter 4: The Wagner Group's Activities in Africa

The Wagner Group's activities in Africa have been the subject of much controversy and speculation. The group's involvement in the continent has been linked to a range of activities, including military operations, resource extraction, and political interference. In this chapter, we will explore the Wagner Group's activities in Africa and examine their implications for regional security and international relations.

Background

The Wagner Group's involvement in Africa dates back to at least 2017 when reports emerged of the group's activities in Sudan. Since then, the group has been linked to a range of activities across the continent, including military operations in Libya and resource extraction in the Central African Republic.

Military Operations in Libya:

The Wagner Group's involvement in the Libyan conflict has been controversial, with the group providing military support to General Khalifa Haftar's Libyan National Army (LNA) in its fight against the UN-backed Government of National Accord (GNA). The group's involvement has been characterized by its use of mercenaries, who are reportedly drawn from countries across Africa, including Sudan, Chad, and Niger.

The Wagner Group's mercenaries are believed to have played a key role in supporting the LNA's military operations, including providing infantry support, artillery fire, and air support. The group has also been accused of committing human rights abuses, including extrajudicial killings and torture. The UN has accused the group of violating the arms embargo on Libya and exacerbating the conflict.

The Wagner Group's involvement in Libya has wider implications for regional security and international relations. The conflict has destabilized the country and fueled regional tensions, with a range of countries involved in supporting different factions. The Wagner Group's involvement in the conflict has raised concerns about the proliferation of weapons and the exacerbation of conflict, which could have wider implications for regional stability.

Resource Extraction in the Central African Republic:

The Wagner Group's involvement in the Central African Republic (CAR) has been linked to its interest in the country's mineral resources, particularly its reserves of diamonds, gold, and uranium. The group has been accused of providing military support to the CAR government in exchange for access to these resources.

The Wagner Group's involvement in the CAR has been controversial, with reports of the group's fighters committing human rights abuses, including sexual violence and forced labor. The group has also been accused of exacerbating the conflict in the country by supporting the government against rebel groups.

The Wagner Group's involvement in the CAR has wider implications for regional security and international relations. The conflict has destabilized the country and fueled regional tensions, with a range of countries involved in supporting different factions. The Wagner Group's involvement in the conflict has raised concerns about the proliferation of weapons and the exacerbation of conflict, which could have wider implications for regional stability.

Political Interference in Sudan:

The Wagner Group's involvement in Sudan has been linked to its interest in securing access to the country's oil reserves. The group has been accused of supporting the

Sudanese government in exchange for access to these resources.

The group's activities in Sudan have also been linked to its interest in political interference in the country. The group has been accused of supporting former President Omar al-Bashir and his regime, which was overthrown in a popular uprising in 2019. The group's involvement in Sudan has raised concerns about political interference and the potential for destabilization in the region.

The Wagner Group's involvement in Sudan has wider implications for regional security and international relations. Sudan is a strategically important country in Africa, and its instability could have wider implications for the region. The Wagner Group's involvement in Sudan highlights Russia's interest in expanding its influence in Africa and its willingness to support authoritarian regimes in pursuit of its strategic goals.

Implications for Regional Security and International Relations:

The Wagner Group's activities in Africa have raised concerns about their impact on regional security and international relations. The group's involvement in conflicts in Libya and the CAR has been linked to the proliferation of weapons and the exacerbation of conflict, which could have wider implications for regional stability.

The group's involvement in Sudan has also raised concerns about political interference and the potential for destabilization in the region. The group's activities in Africa have also been linked to Russia's wider foreign policy, particularly its interest in expanding its influence in the continent.

The Wagner Group's activities in Africa highlight the challenges posed by the growing involvement of private military companies in conflicts around the world. Private military companies operate outside of traditional state structures, raising concerns about accountability and transparency.

Conclusion

The Wagner Group's activities in Africa have been diverse and multifaceted, with the group involved in military operations, resource extraction, and political interference. The group's involvement in conflicts in Libya and the CAR has been particularly controversial, with concerns about human rights abuses and the exacerbation of conflict. The group's activities in Africa have wider implications for regional security and international relations, and they highlight the challenges posed by the growing involvement of private military companies in conflicts around the world.

Chapter 5: The Wagner Group's Role in Russian Foreign Policy

The Wagner Group's activities are closely tied to Russia's foreign policy objectives, particularly in regions of strategic importance such as Syria, Ukraine, and Africa. The group is believed to have close links to the Russian government and has been described as a "private army" that operates in support of Russian foreign policy goals. In this chapter, we will examine the Wagner Group's role in Russian foreign policy and its implications for international relations.

Syria:

The Wagner Group's involvement in Syria is closely linked to Russia's strategic interests in the Middle East. Russia has been a key ally of the Syrian government, providing military and political support in the country's long-running civil war. The Wagner Group's mercenaries have played a key role in supporting the Syrian government's military operations, including providing infantry support, artillery fire, and air support. The group's involvement has enabled Russia to support the Syrian government without committing its troops and has been described as a "low-cost, low-risk" option for Russia.

The Wagner Group's involvement in Syria has wider implications for Russian foreign policy and international relations. Russia's support for the Syrian government has put it at odds with the international community, particularly the United States and its allies. The Wagner Group's involvement in the conflict has also raised concerns about human rights abuses, particularly the group's reported use of chemical weapons. The conflict in Syria has fueled regional tensions and has been linked to the growth of extremist groups such as ISIS.

Ukraine:

The Wagner Group's involvement in the conflict in eastern Ukraine is closely tied to Russia's interest in maintaining influence in the country. Russia has been accused of supporting separatist groups in the Donbas region, providing military and political support to the self-proclaimed Donetsk and Luhansk People's Republics. The Wagner Group's mercenaries have been accused of playing a key role in supporting these separatist groups, providing infantry support, artillery fire, and other military capabilities.

Russia's involvement in the conflict in Ukraine has wider implications for international relations and regional security. The conflict has fueled tensions between Russia and the West, particularly the United States and its allies. The conflict has also raised concerns about the proliferation of weapons and the exacerbation of regional tensions.

Africa:

The Wagner Group's involvement in Africa is closely tied to Russia's interest in expanding its influence on the continent. Russia has been accused of using the Wagner Group to support authoritarian regimes and to gain access to strategic resources such as oil and minerals. The group's involvement in conflicts in Libya, the Central African Republic, and Sudan has raised concerns about the proliferation of weapons and the exacerbation of conflict in the region.

Russia's involvement in Africa has wider implications for international relations and regional security. The growth of Russia's influence in Africa has put it at odds with Western countries, particularly the United States and its allies. The Wagner Group's activities in Africa have also raised concerns about the proliferation of weapons and the exacerbation of conflict, which could have wider implications for regional stability.

Implications for International Relations:

The Wagner Group's activities have wider implications for international relations and the role of private military companies in global conflicts. The group's close links to the Russian government raise questions about the use of private military companies as a tool of state policy. The group's involvement in conflicts around the world has raised concerns about the proliferation of weapons, human rights abuses, and the exacerbation of conflict, which could have wider implications for regional security and international stability.

The Wagner Group's activities have also highlighted the challenges of regulating private military companies in global conflicts. Private military companies operate outside of traditional state structures and are subject to limited regulation, raising concerns about accountability and transparency. The growth of private military companies has challenged traditional notions of state sovereignty and has raised questions about the legitimacy of their actions in global conflicts.

The Wagner Group's activities have also highlighted the growing importance of non-state actors in global conflicts. Private military companies such as the Wagner Group have become an increasingly important tool for states and non-state actors to achieve their strategic objectives, often operating outside of traditional state structures and with limited accountability.

The Wagner Group's involvement in conflicts around the world has also raised concerns about the use of mercenaries and the erosion of the state monopoly on violence. The use of mercenaries has been linked to human rights abuses and the proliferation of weapons, which could have wider implications for regional stability and international security.

The Wagner Group's activities have also raised questions about the role of Russia in global conflicts and its relationship with the international community. Russia's support for the Wagner Group has put it at odds with Western countries, particularly the United States and its allies. The Wagner Group's activities have also raised concerns about Russia's use of non-state actors to achieve its strategic objectives and the implications for international relations.

Conclusion:

The Wagner Group's activities are closely tied to Russia's foreign policy objectives, particularly in regions of strategic importance such as Syria, Ukraine, and Africa. The group's involvement in conflicts around the world has raised concerns about the use of private military companies, the erosion of the state monopoly on violence, and the proliferation of weapons. The group's activities have also highlighted the growing importance of non-state actors in global conflicts and the challenges of regulating their actions.

The Wagner Group's activities have wider implications for international relations and regional security, particularly in the Middle East and Africa. The group's involvement in conflicts has put Russia at odds with the international community and has raised concerns about its relationship with non-state actors. The implications of the Wagner Group's activities for global security and stability are complex and far-reaching and will require careful consideration by policymakers and scholars alike.

Chapter 6: The Wagner Group's Expansion and Global Reach

Introduction:

The Wagner Group's expansion and global reach have been a significant development in the world of private military companies. While the group's activities have primarily focused on conflicts in Syria and Ukraine, its operations have extended to other regions of the world, including Africa and South America. This chapter will examine the Wagner Group's expansion and global reach, including its operations in other regions and its future ambitions.

Operations in South America:

The Wagner Group's activities in South America have been more limited than its operations in other regions. However, the group has reportedly been involved in operations in Venezuela, supporting the government of Nicolas Maduro. The group's involvement in Venezuela has raised concerns about Russia's influence in the region and its relationship with non-state actors.

The operations in South America have primarily been focused on supporting the government of Nicolas Maduro in Venezuela. The group's involvement in Venezuela has been linked to Russia's broader geopolitical ambitions in the region, as it seeks to establish a foothold in South America and counter the influence of the United States.

In early 2019, reports emerged that the Wagner Group had deployed a group of mercenaries to Venezuela to provide security for Maduro's regime. The group was reportedly tasked with protecting the country's oil infrastructure and supporting government forces in the event of a coup attempt or foreign intervention. The Wagner Group's involvement in Venezuela has been significant, as it has provided the government with a powerful tool to suppress opposition and maintain power.

The Wagner Group's operations in Venezuela have raised concerns about Russia's influence in the region, particularly as the country has been mired in a political and economic crisis for several years. The group's activities have also highlighted the growing use of private military companies to achieve strategic objectives and the potential implications for global security and stability.

The specifics of the Wagner Group's operations in South America, and in Venezuela specifically, are somewhat unclear. The group operates with a high degree of secrecy and operates outside of traditional state structures, making it difficult to verify its activities. However, reports indicate that the Wagner Group has been involved in training and supporting government forces in Venezuela, and has played a significant role in maintaining the Maduro regime's grip on power.

The Wagner Group's activities in South America are likely to continue to be a source of concern for policymakers and scholars alike. The group's involvement in Venezuela has highlighted the growing use of non-state actors in global conflicts and the implications for state sovereignty and international relations. As Russia seeks to expand its influence in South America, the Wagner Group will likely play an increasingly important role in the region.

Future Ambitions:

The Wagner Group's future ambitions are not entirely clear, but there are several indications of their continued expansion and growth. It is believed that they will continue to expand their operations and influence in Africa, particularly in countries where there is a high demand for security services and a lack of regulation in the sector. They have already established a strong presence in Libya, the Central African Republic, and Sudan, and there are indications that they may be looking to expand into other countries in the region.

In addition to Africa, the Wagner Group may also be looking to expand its operations in other parts of the world. There have been reports of their involvement in South America, particularly in Venezuela, where they have been providing security services to the government of Nicolas Maduro. There are also reports that they may be looking to expand their operations in Asia, particularly in Myanmar, where there is a need for security services amid ongoing conflict and instability.

It is unclear how the Wagner Group will continue to grow and expand, given the increasing scrutiny and criticism they have faced from the international community. However, it is clear that they are a powerful and influential force in the world of private military contractors, and they are likely to continue to play a significant role in conflicts and political crises around the world. As long as there is demand for their services and a lack of regulation in the sector, the Wagner Group is likely to continue to thrive and expand its operations.

Conclusion:

The Wagner Group's expansion and global reach have been a significant development in the world of private military companies. The group's activities in Africa and South America have raised concerns about Russia's influence in these regions, while its involvement in conflicts in Syria and Ukraine has highlighted the growing importance of non-state actors in global conflicts. The Wagner Group's future ambitions are likely to continue to shape Russia's foreign policy and its relationship with the international community.

Chapter 7: The Wagner Group's Relationship with the Russian Government

The Wagner Group is a private military company that has been linked to the Russian government. Despite the lack of official acknowledgment or endorsement, the group's activities appear to align with Russia's broader geopolitical objectives, particularly in regions such as Syria, Ukraine, and Venezuela. This chapter will explore the relationship between the Wagner Group and the Russian government, and the implications for global security and stability.

The origins of the Wagner Group are somewhat murky, but it is widely believed to have been founded by Yevgeny Prigozhin, a close ally of Russian President Vladimir Putin. Prigozhin, who has been dubbed "Putin's chef" due to his catering businesses, has been linked to several Russian military operations in recent years, including the annexation of Crimea and the war in Syria.

While the Russian government has not officially acknowledged its relationship with the Wagner Group, there is evidence to suggest that the group enjoys a degree of support and protection from the Russian state. For example, some reports suggest that the group operates with the tacit approval of the Kremlin and that its members receive training and support from Russian military personnel. In addition, there have been reports of Russian soldiers being killed while fighting alongside Wagner Group mercenaries in Syria and Ukraine, suggesting a level of coordination and cooperation between the two groups.

The exact nature of the relationship between the Wagner Group and the Russian government is difficult to ascertain, due to the lack of transparency and official acknowledgment. However, it is clear that the group's activities align with Russia's broader geopolitical objectives, particularly in regions where the Kremlin seeks to expand its influence and counter the influence of the United States and its allies.

In Syria, for example, the Wagner Group has been instrumental in supporting the government of President Bashar al-Assad, which is backed by Russia. The group has been linked to several high-profile military operations in the country, including the recapture of the city of Palmyra in 2016. The group's involvement in Syria has raised concerns about the use of private military companies to achieve strategic objectives and the implications for state sovereignty and international relations.

Similarly, in Ukraine, the Wagner Group has been linked to Russia's annexation of Crimea and the ongoing conflict in the eastern part of the country. The group's activities in Ukraine have been characterized by a high degree of secrecy and deniability, with Russian officials denying any involvement in the conflict. However, there is evidence to suggest that the group has been providing military support to separatist groups in the region, including training and equipment.

The Wagner Group's relationship with the Russian government raises important questions about the use of private military companies to achieve strategic objectives and the implications for global security and stability. The group's activities appear to align with Russia's broader geopolitical ambitions, particularly in regions where the Kremlin seeks to expand its influence and counter the influence of the United States and its allies.

The use of private military companies also raises concerns about state sovereignty and international law. Private military companies operate outside of traditional state structures, making it difficult to hold them accountable for their actions. This raises questions about the legality of their activities and the potential for abuse and human rights violations.

In conclusion, the Wagner Group's relationship with the Russian government is a complex and opaque issue. While the exact nature of the relationship is difficult to ascertain, it is clear that the group's activities align with Russia's broader geopolitical objectives. The use of private military companies to achieve strategic objectives raises important questions about state sovereignty, international law, and global security and stability. As such, the relationship between the Wagner Group and the Russian government is likely to remain a source of concern for policymakers and scholars alike.

Chapter 8: Controversies and Criticisms

Wagner Group, a private military company (PMC) based in Russia, has been involved in various military conflicts and operations around the world, often in support of Russian interests. The company has gained notoriety and has been the subject of controversies and criticisms for its actions and operations. In this chapter, we will discuss some of the controversies and criticisms surrounding the Wagner Group.

Controversies and Criticisms

1. Lack of Transparency and Legal Status:

One of the primary criticisms leveled against the Wagner Group is the lack of transparency and legal status of the company. As a PMC, the Wagner Group operates outside the legal framework of most countries, including Russia. This lack of transparency has made it difficult for governments and international organizations to monitor the company's actions and hold it accountable for any violations of international law or human rights.

2. Involvement in Conflict Zones:

The Wagner Group has been involved in numerous conflicts around the world, often in support of Russian interests. The group's involvement in Ukraine, Syria, and Libya has been particularly controversial, as it has been accused of committing war crimes and other violations of international law. The company's activities in these conflict zones have raised concerns about its impact on regional stability and the potential for escalation of violence.

3. Allegations of Human Rights Violations:

The Wagner Group has been accused of numerous human rights violations, including torture, extrajudicial killings, and forced disappearances. In Syria, the company has been accused of carrying out attacks on civilian populations, including the use of chemical weapons. In Libya, the company has been accused of recruiting child soldiers and carrying out executions.

4. Lack of Accountability:

One of the main criticisms of the Wagner Group is the lack of accountability for its actions. As a PMC, the company operates outside the legal framework of most countries and is not subject to the same regulations and oversight as national militaries. This lack of accountability has made it difficult to hold the company responsible for any violations of international law or human rights.

5. Alleged Ties to the Russian Government:

The Wagner Group has been linked to the Russian government, and some have suggested that the company operates as a proxy for the Russian military. This alleged connection has raised concerns about the Russian government's involvement in conflicts around the world and the potential for the company's actions to escalate into larger geopolitical conflicts.

6. Impact on Regional Stability:

The Wagner Group's involvement in conflicts around the world has raised concerns about its impact on regional stability. The company's activities have been linked to the ongoing conflict in Ukraine and the civil war in Syria, and its involvement in Libya has been criticized for exacerbating the country's instability. The company's actions have also raised concerns about the potential for escalation of violence and conflict in the regions where it operates.

7. Negative Perception of Private Military Companies:

The use of private military companies has been a controversial issue in international affairs, with some arguing that their use undermines the traditional role of national militaries and raises concerns about accountability and oversight. The Wagner Group's actions and controversies have contributed to a negative perception of private military companies and raised questions about their role in global security.

Another area of controversy surrounding the Wagner Group is its treatment of its own soldiers. Reports have emerged that the group recruits mercenaries, particularly from economically deprived areas in Russia and Ukraine, with promises of high pay and benefits, only to abandon them in conflict zones without proper equipment or medical care. The group has been accused of leaving wounded soldiers to die and failing to provide compensation or support to the families of deceased soldiers.

In addition to its treatment of soldiers, the Wagner Group has also been accused of committing war crimes and human rights violations in conflict zones. In Syria, the group has been accused of being involved in the chemical attack on Douma in 2018, which led to international condemnation and retaliatory airstrikes by the United States, the United Kingdom, and France. The group has also been accused of using torture, rape, and murder as tools of intimidation and control in conflict zones.

The Wagner Group's activities have also been a source of tension between Russia and other countries. In Libya, the group's support for Haftar's forces has been seen as undermining efforts to establish a stable and democratic government in the country. The group's involvement in the Central African Republic has been criticized for fueling conflict and exacerbating the country's humanitarian crisis.

The group's relationship with the Russian government has also been a source of controversy. While the Russian government has denied any official links to the group, many experts believe that the group is supported by the Russian military and intelligence agencies. The group's activities have been seen as a means for the Russian government to project power and influence in conflict zones without the risk of direct involvement.

Despite the controversies and criticism, the Wagner Group continues to operate and expand its reach. The group's future ambitions are unclear, but it will likely continue to seek out new opportunities for expansion and influence in conflict zones around the world. The group's activities will remain a source of concern for international security and human rights organizations, as well as for countries that seek to promote stability and democracy in conflict zones.

Chapter 9: Current Status and Future Prospects

As of 2023, the Wagner Group remains active and involved in conflicts and operations around the world. The group has expanded its reach beyond its origins in eastern Ukraine and Syria and is now involved in conflicts and operations in Africa, South America, and other parts of the world. Despite facing significant criticism and controversy, the group appears to have continued support from the Russian government, which has allowed it to operate with relative impunity.

The group's future prospects are uncertain, as it faces significant challenges both domestically and internationally. Domestically, the group's lack of transparency and accountability has led to calls for greater regulation and oversight, as well as investigations into its funding and ownership structure. Internationally, the group's involvement in conflicts and operations has led to significant criticism and condemnation from the international community, as well as sanctions from the US and European Union.

Despite these challenges, the Wagner Group remains a significant player in global conflicts and operations and is likely to continue to be involved in such activities in the future. The group's experience and expertise in military and security operations, as well as its connections to the Russian government, make it a valuable asset for those seeking to engage in covert or deniable operations.

However, the group's reputation has been significantly damaged by its involvement in war crimes and human rights abuses, which could limit its future prospects. The international community has become increasingly vocal in its condemnation of such activities, and there are growing calls for greater accountability for those responsible.

In the future, the Wagner Group may face increased pressure to operate within the bounds of international law and norms, as well as greater scrutiny and regulation from the Russian government. The group may also face greater competition from other private military and security companies, which are increasingly active in global conflicts and operations.

Overall, the current status and future prospects of the Wagner Group are complex and uncertain. The group remains a significant player in global conflicts and operations but faces significant challenges and criticisms. Its future trajectory will depend on a range of factors, including international politics, regulation and oversight, and the willingness of the group's leaders to adhere to international norms and standards.

Trajectory

2014:

- The Wagner Group is founded by Yevgeny Prigozhin, a businessman with close ties to the Russian government.

- The group is initially involved in providing security for Russian businesses operating in conflict zones.

2015:

- The group becomes involved in the conflict in eastern Ukraine, fighting alongside pro-Russian separatists.

- Reports emerge of the group's involvement in the conflict, but the Russian government denies any official links to the group.

2016:

- The group becomes involved in the Syrian civil war, fighting on behalf of the Assad regime.

- Reports emerge of the group's involvement in Syria, but the Russian government denies any official links to the group.

2017:

- The group is accused of involvement in the conflict in Libya, providing support for forces loyal to General Khalifa Haftar.

2018:

- The group is accused of being involved in the chemical attack on Douma, Syria, which leads to international condemnation and retaliatory airstrikes by the United States, the United Kingdom, and France.

2019:

- The group becomes involved in the conflict in the Central African Republic, providing support for the government of President Faustin-Archange Touadéra.

2020:

- Reports emerge of the group's involvement in the conflict between Armenia and Azerbaijan over Nagorno-Karabakh, with the group allegedly providing support for Azerbaijan.

- The group is accused of being involved in the coup in Mali, with reports suggesting that the group provided support for the military junta that seized power.

2021:

- The group becomes involved in the conflict in Mozambique, providing support for government forces against Islamist militants.

- The group is accused of being involved in the coup in Sudan, with reports suggesting that the group provided support for the military junta that seized power.

- The group's leader, Yevgeny Prigozhin, is sanctioned by the United States government for his alleged involvement in the Wagner Group's activities.

The Wagner Group's activities have been shrouded in secrecy, and the group has likely been involved in other conflicts and activities that have not been publicly reported. Despite international criticism and sanctions, the group continues to operate and expand its reach, and its future activities and ambitions remain a source of concern for international security and human rights organizations.

About the Author

Sahil A Gosalia is a renowned author and a passionate researcher in the field of global security and international relations. He has written extensively on the subject of private military companies and their role in conflict zones around the world. With a deep understanding of the complexities of geopolitics and security, he has provided valuable insights into the workings of the Wagner Group and its relationship with the Russian government.

As a prolific writer, Sahil A Gosalia has published several articles and papers on the topic of private military companies and their impact on global security. He is known for his in-depth analysis and his ability to bring to light the hidden workings of secretive organizations like the Wagner Group.

He has always been fascinated by secretive organizations and their operations. He believes that these organizations have a significant impact on global affairs and that understanding their workings is crucial to understanding the world we live in. His fascination with secretive stuff led him to research the Wagner Group, one of the most secretive and controversial private military companies in the world.

Sahil A Gosalia's deep interest in the subject has enabled him to uncover important insights into the Wagner Group's operations and its relationship with the Russian government. His research has shed light on the workings of this secretive organization and has provided valuable information to policymakers and scholars alike.

Notes

Notes

Notes

Scan to check more of my work!

Scan to BUY Books, Journals, Notebooks

Scan to BUY Kindle Edition E-Books

Scan to know more about the Author

Printed in Great Britain
by Amazon

21441520R00072